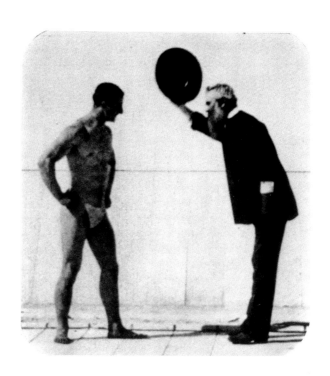

The magic of photography is metaphysical.
What you see in the photograph
isn't what you saw at the time.
The real skill of photography
is organised visual lying.

TERENCE DONOVAN

PORTRAITS
A Book of Photographs by Peter McWilliams
Copyright ©1992 by Peter McWilliams

Prelude Press
8159 Santa Moncia Blvd.
Los Angeles, California 90046

Cover Design: Paul LeBus
Book Design: Paul LeBus
Desktop Publishing: Karen Maria Rufa
Printed and Manufactured in the United States

❧

Other books by Peter McWilliams published by Prelude Press
I Marry You Because
Come Love With Me & Be My Life
The Personal Computer Book

with John-Roger:
LIFE 101: Everything We Wish We Had Learned About Life In School—But Didn't
The Portable LIFE 101
DO IT! Let's Get Off Our Buts
You Can't Afford the Luxury of a Negative Thought
Focus on the Positive
WEALTH 101: Getting What You Want—Enjoying What You've Got

with Melba Colgrove, Ph.D., and Harold H. Bloomfield, M.D.:
How to Survive the Loss of a Love
Surviving, Healing & Growing: The How to Survive the Loss of a Love Workbook

❧

My thanks to Paul LeBus and Christopher McMullen
for their invaluable help in selecting the photos, and to my brother, Michael, for liking them.
Thanks to Mom and Aunt Net for the Family Photo Archives.

❧

This book is dedicated to Maurice, Paul and Christopher, with love.

PORTRAITS

A BOOK OF PHOTOGRAPHS BY
PETER McWILLIAMS

*Photography is a tool for dealing
with things everybody knows about
but isn't attending to.*

EMMET GOWIN

*The photographer is like the cod,
which produces a million eggs in order
that one may reach maturity.*

GEORGE BERNARD SHAW

*I am a camera with its shutter open,
quite passive, recording, not thinking.
Recording the man shaving at the window opposite
and the woman in the kimono washing her hair.
Some day, all this will have to be developed,
carefully printed, fixed.*

CHRISTOPHER ISHERWOOD
*A Berlin Diary
Autumn, 1930*

To photograph truthfully and effectively
is to see beneath the surfaces and
record the qualities of nature and humanity
which live or are latent in all things.

ANSEL ADAMS

❧

Photography records the gamut of feelings
written on the human face,
the beauty of the earth and skies
that man has inherited,
and the wealth and confusion
man has created.
It is a major force
in explaining man to man.

EDWARD STEICHEN

❧

Photography is the
"art form"
of the untalented.

GORE VIDAL

INTRODUCTION:

Photography & Me—Photography & Pre-Me

I have been taking pictures as long as I can remember. But why? What started it? And why photography?

For the answers to these questions, I did some research in the Family Photo Archives (those four end-table drawers in my mother's living room where the photos were always stored).

There is nothing in my background that, on the surface, would make me a photographer. I am a fairly typical card-carrying member of the Baby Boom generation. My father went to war, returned to find his then-wife *not* waiting for him, met my mother and got married in 1946. They spent three enjoyable years together—and then I came along.

I grew up in Allen Park, Michigan, an ordinary post-war suburb of Detroit. Detroit is not known for producing photographers. Detroit produces cars and entertainers. (Tom Selleck, Diana Ross, Lily Tomlin. Lily was once asked, "When did you leave Detroit?" She answered, "When I found out where I was.")

I was once told by a psychic that I was a painter in a past life. There, he told me, I learned about framing, cropping, choosing subject matter and all the things central to photography. Be that as it may, I certainly took no *drawing* ability from that—or any other—lifetime.

Thank heavens for photography. It nicely balances, on one hand, my love of beauty and fascination for things mechanical with, on the other, my impatience and complete inability to draw.

Going through the Family Photo Archives, one need not go to a past life to find an appreciation for beautiful pictures. Mom and Dad both seemed to have it. And they created some beautiful pictures themselves.

*My father (seated, right) on Miami Beach: "Xmas day 1926," his notation reads. He was twenty —
the same age my mother would be when they met, twenty years later.*

In 1946, my father met my mother. He was supervisor for a drug chain in Detroit. She was making Easter baskets for that chain. He was twice as old as she.

Here's a remarkable photograph my father took of my mother in 1947, before she was my (or anyone else's) mother. It's far superior to the standard snapshot of the day. Why is there so much white space? Why was it taken from such a distance? And what is the expression on my mother's face? I can't find words for it. Does it have anything to do with the handkerchief in her hand? I don't know.

The shadow on the ground is my father. He is holding a Kodak Brownie box camera at waist level, looking down. With this camera you looked down to frame the shot in front of you. It was cumbersome, inaccurate, silly and prone to tilted photos. (All of this is a justification for the Leaning-Tower-of-Pisa quality of my first photos, which we'll get to shortly.)

I found precisely this camera in a vintage Sears Roebuck catalog—from 1927! Even then it was "well-known." By measuring the negatives, I figured out the camera my parents had was the No. 2A—$3.19 in 1927. It lasted well into the '60s.

Here's a photograph of my father's two primary passions at the time—my mother and his car. (Unusual: photographing someone walking on a car. Unusual, too, in that my father barely let people ride in his car, much less walk on it.)

My mother, as photographed by my father, amidst nature.

My mother, my father's shadow, and my father's sister, Monnetta. (Aunt Net's Family Photo Archives contributed to this Introduction as well. Thanks Aunt Net!) Note the interesting architectural formation on the right—fully included in the photograph.

My dad, as photographed by my mom, on a visit home. He was proud of his home state, and proud of his new wife.

Mother either did not enjoy her visit, or she was getting tired of that dress.

It must have been the dress. Here she is with a new dress and a new fishing pole—happy and Southern (as Southern as a girl from Detroit can be), looking like something out of Tennessee Williams.

An idyllic nature scene with my father (right) and my godfather, who shall remain nameless, because I don't remember seeing him once in my life—especially on those important occasions when a child needs a godfather most: birthdays and Christmas. Still, it's a beautiful picture my mom took.

Another of my mother's artistic photographs. Here's a picture she took of my father in 1948 that is so artistic it's almost surreal. (By the way, on either side of the couch are the two end tables that became the Family Photo Archives.)

Some photo subjects must be hereditary. To the right is a picture of my father (center), his brother Cletus (covering the "WO") and Cletus' son, taken by my mother in 1947.

Below is a photo I took of my mother and her mother twenty-four years later (1971).

The joyful post-war, post-marriage, pre-me days came to an end on August 5, 1949. (I'm the one on the right.)

Although there were diapers to change, bottles to warm and (shortly) putting-all-breakable-objects-on-high-places-not-near-any-chairs-or-anything-I-could-climb-on, Mother still found time for artful photography.

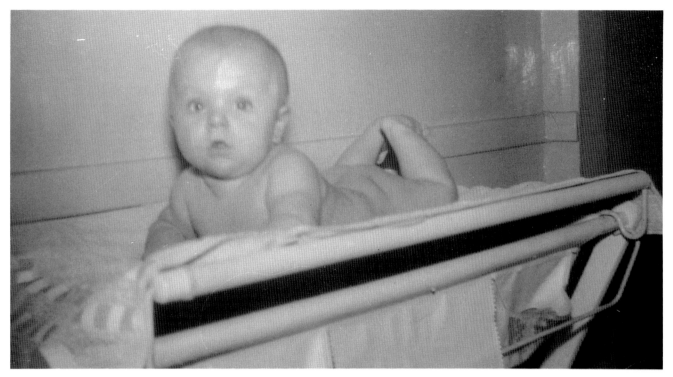

Here, the heart of art—the nude. A rear...

...and a partial-frontal.

Before I was six months old, I could do—on command—three imitations: crocodile (moving my jaw from side to side), Tarzan (beating my chest) and Mussolini (raising my chin in an arrogant pout). As you can see from this photograph, Mussolini was the most convincing. I looked remarkably like him.

And the old ashtray-on-the-head-while-dancing-to-Japanese-Sandman routine never failed to wow them. (Think I looked a little like Jack Nicholson?)

Here's my favorite photo of childhood. By ignoring the standard advice, "Never point your camera toward the sun," Mother discovered her own form of backlighting.

It's my second Christmas, and I'm sixteen months old. This photo demonstrates that in a photograph, expression is more important than technical perfection—a lesson I learned well from Mom.

Of this photo my mother wrote almost forty years later, "I love that expression! It seems like you are deciding whether or not to remove a bulb."

Season's Greetings

THE McWILLIAMS

MARY · MAC · PETER

Perhaps inspired by the previous two pictures, the next year Mom and Dad began a family tradition— the Photo Christmas Card.

Above, I am not yet two-and-a-half, in a suit given to me by my grandmother for my second birthday. The male and female styrofoam snow-persons were, I suppose, to represent Mom and Dad.

Merry Christmas
Happy New Year

The Mc Williams

The next year, the same suit but a new baby brother, Michael. That thing behind him that looks as though it's made from ten thousand pipe cleaners is the Christmas tree. The early '50s were a strange time.

By 1955, my brother had inherited my suit and learned how to talk. The Photo Christmas Card had become a real production number. Note the prop tree, prop Santa, prop fireplace—even prop fire. Mother would go through roll after roll of film. Flash bulbs flashed. Tempers flared. Models became irritable. It was a regular photo session.

The next year we had a prop organ. On these pages are three out-takes from Christmas, 1956. My mother couldn't resist going for the expressions. As much trouble as these photo sessions were, my parents seemed to love them. They would spend hours going over the pictures, selecting the right one. The praise they got was much appreciated.

By this time, however, I had gotten into the act. The ash tray no longer fit my head. I looked more like Fanny Brice than Mussolini. So, I took up photography.

Here (ta da!) is my first photograph. It was taken just before my sixth birthday. I don't remember taking it, but it's obviously mine. First, it's taken at an angle roughly three feet off the ground—the height at which I would have held the camera at the time. Second, I'm not in the picture. Third, the camera tilts violently to the left, the sign of a five-year-old trying to master a box camera.

By the time I got around to my second photograph, later that day, I had learned four important lessons. First, hold the camera straighter. Second, hold the camera stiller. ("The principal thing to learn in using the Kodak is to hold it steady," as the book Kodak Man stated in 1890.) Third, limit your subjects to one. Fourth, if you want to use other people's cameras, offer to take their picture.

I eventually got my own camera, a Kodak Brownie Starflash. It was for my ninth birthday. It took square pictures. Imagine: the world of movies had gone wide screen, but the world of photography went square.

I did the best I could, however, to not take square pictures—square in the '50s sense of the term.

Here's how I covered a family picnic when I was nine. I'm proud that there's not a typical gather-'round-and-smile-at-the-camera snapshot in the bunch.

No one was safe—anywhere—from having his or her "portrait" taken by me. Here's mother, up on the roof.

My taste for the unusual and offbeat began to enter my photos. Here's my brother with his then-girlfriend Cindy. It was their First Communion, but I posed them as though for a Munchkin wedding.

My photos of the unusual continued. As an example of the offbeat—nay, silly—I submit this 1980 photograph, entitled "Fly contemplates suicide." This photograph is probably not quite what Ansel Adams meant when he said, "Sometimes I do get to places just when God's ready to have somebody click the shutter," but for me, it is a similar sensation.

I also have my requisite pictures of Nature, although I seem to prefer something human-made in the landscape—especially when that human-made object is busy being reclaimed by nature, such as this house trailer in New Mexico.

But this is a book of the portraits.

It is my sincere wish that you enjoy them.

The great photographer, Edward Muybridge, meeting a model. San Francisco, 1879.

One hundred years later, yours truly (right) meeting a model, Hollywood style.

About the Photographs

For the most part, a photograph must stand—or fall—on its own; hence, no further captions. The pictures that might be enhanced by a word or two of explanation are listed in the Appendix (page 251).

These pictures (not including those in the Introduction) span twenty-two years—1970 to 1992.

I have separated the black & white portraits from the color ones. My eye has difficulty adjusting between black & white and color photography. They are so distinct, they almost seem to be two different art forms. As you can tell from the number of black & white vs. color portraits (roughly a three-to-one ratio), black & white is my favorite.

All photographs (again, excluding those in the Introduction) are 35mm. The cameras used were Nikon F3s with Nikkor 85mm 1.4 portrait lenses (I've gone through several) and a Contax RTS with a Carl Zeiss 85mm 1.4 T* lens. The black & white film is Kodak Plus-X (ASA 125), Tri-X (ASA 400) and, more recently, T-Max (ASA 100 and 400). There are a few rolls of Illford in there, too. The color film is Ektachrome or Kodachrome.

I have not been in a darkroom since I was ten. Ansel Adams forgive me, but I consider photography and lab work two distinct arts, and I do not practice the latter. (Some will say I do not practice the former, either.) Most of the black & white developing was done by Alan's Custom Lab in Hollywood, and all the black & white reproduction prints for this book were personally made by Alan K. Wedertz himself. I am indebted to him for the brilliant practice of his art.

There are no "lab tricks" or retouching on the black & white photographs. People are as they are. The double-exposures or other effects were done in-camera (usually a lucky accident). A handful of the color portraits received minor deblemishing.

Information on ordering prints of any of the black & white photographs can be found on page 250.

Thank you.

—Peter McWilliams
Los Angeles, California
August, 1992

PORTRAITS
A BOOK OF PHOTOGRAPHS
BY PETER MCWILLIAMS

I got your photograph at last:
it is a beastly thing—not a bit like.

EDWARD FITZGERALD
1850

I want to do a large photograph
of Tennyson and he objects!
Says I make bags under his eyes.

WILLIAM ALLINGHAM
1867

We protest:
This isn't me.

GRAHAM GREENE
1943

God knew seventy-seven years ago
that someday I would be pope.
Why couldn't he have made me
a little more photogenic!

POPE JOHN XXIII

THE BLACK & WHITE
PORTRAITS

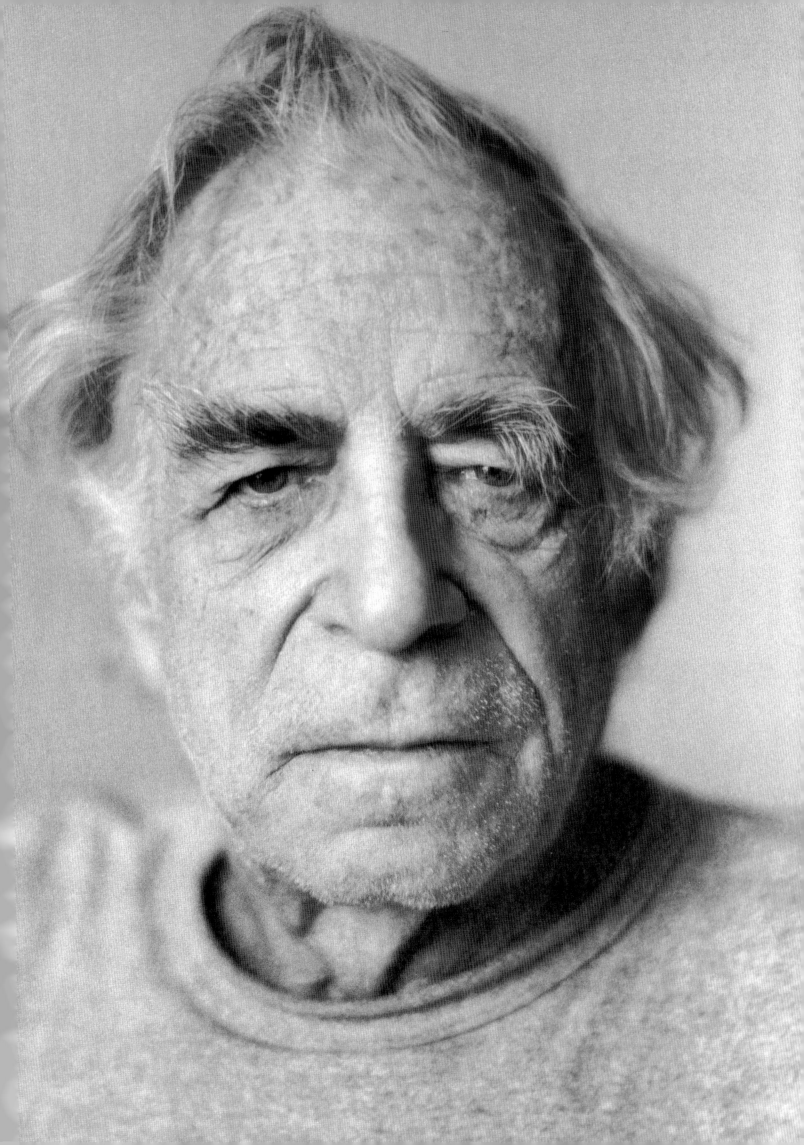

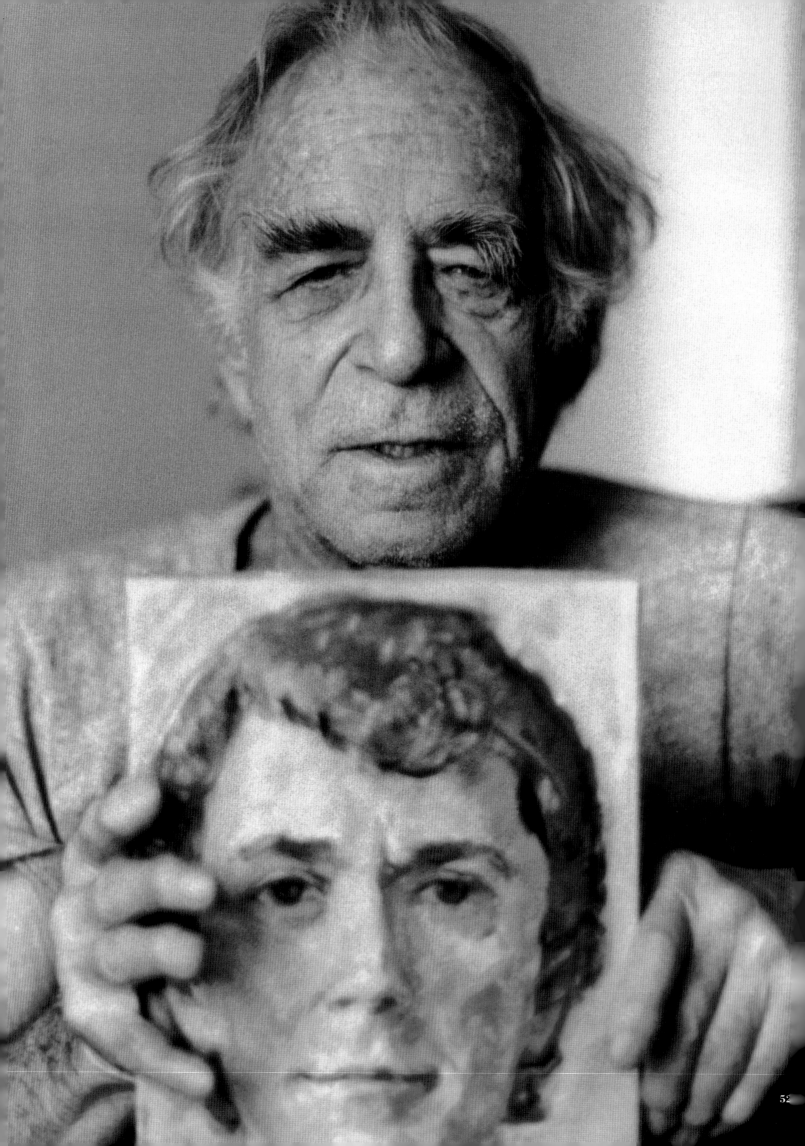

70

76

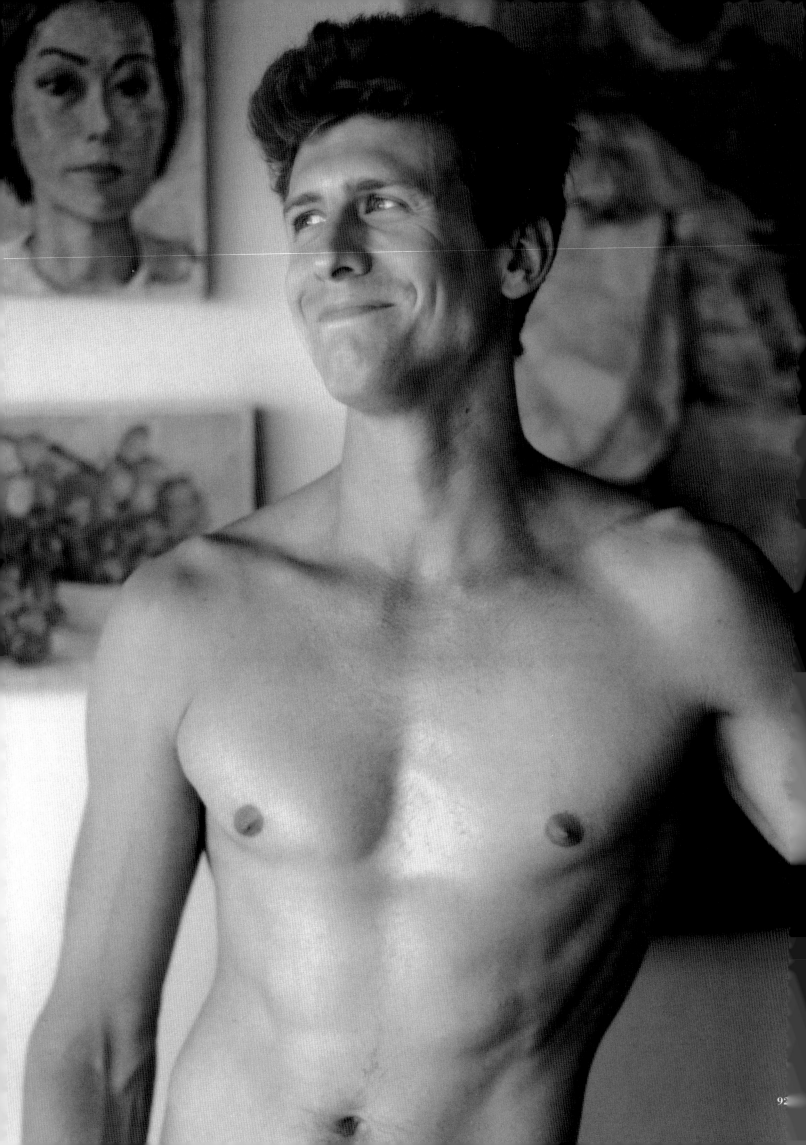

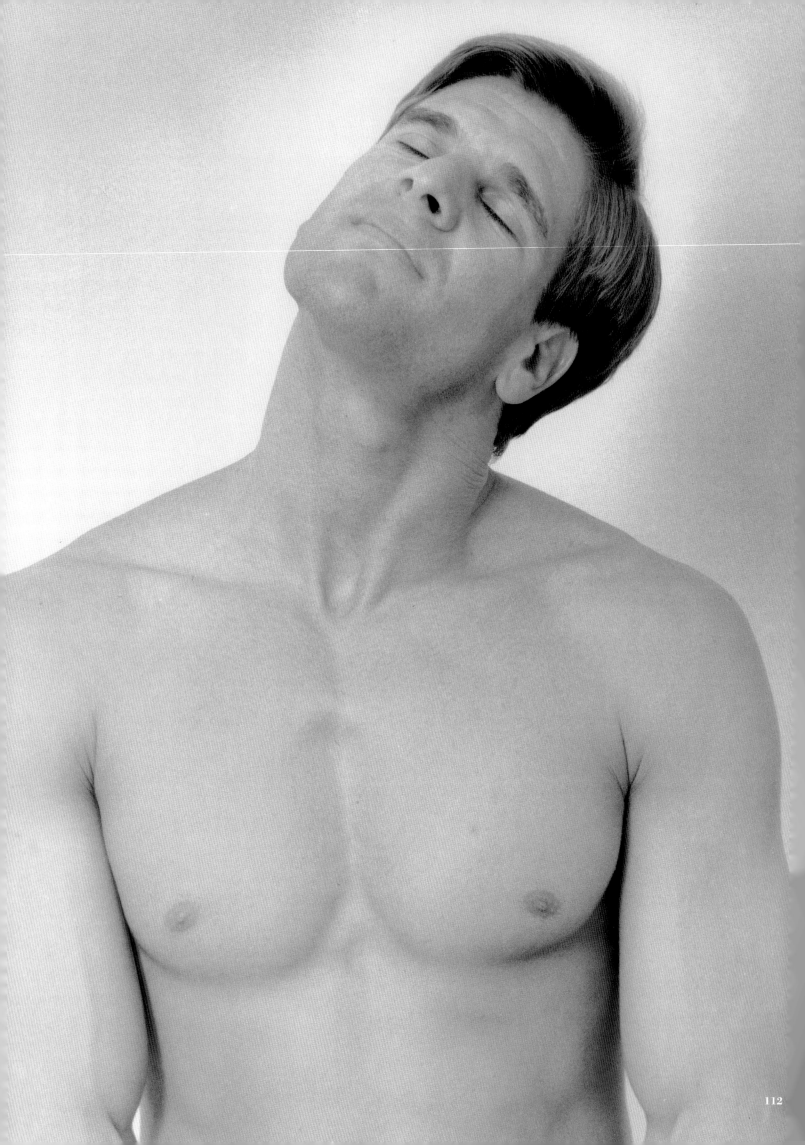

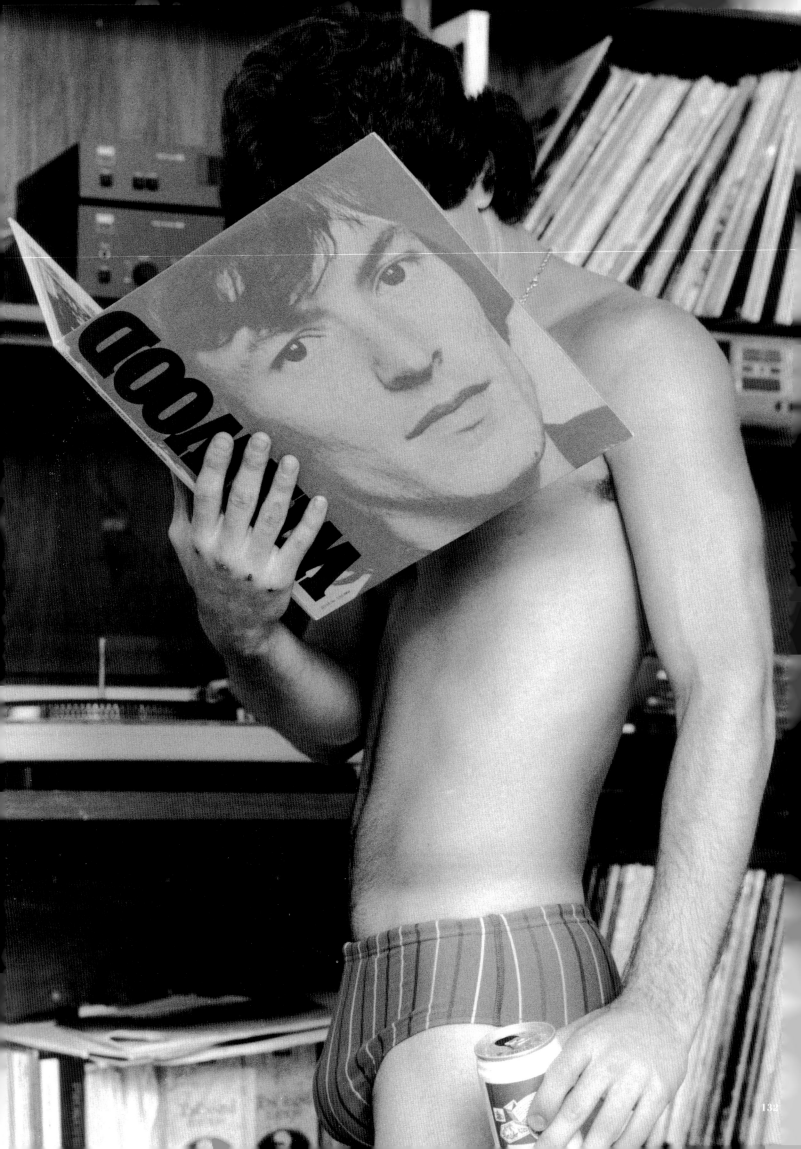

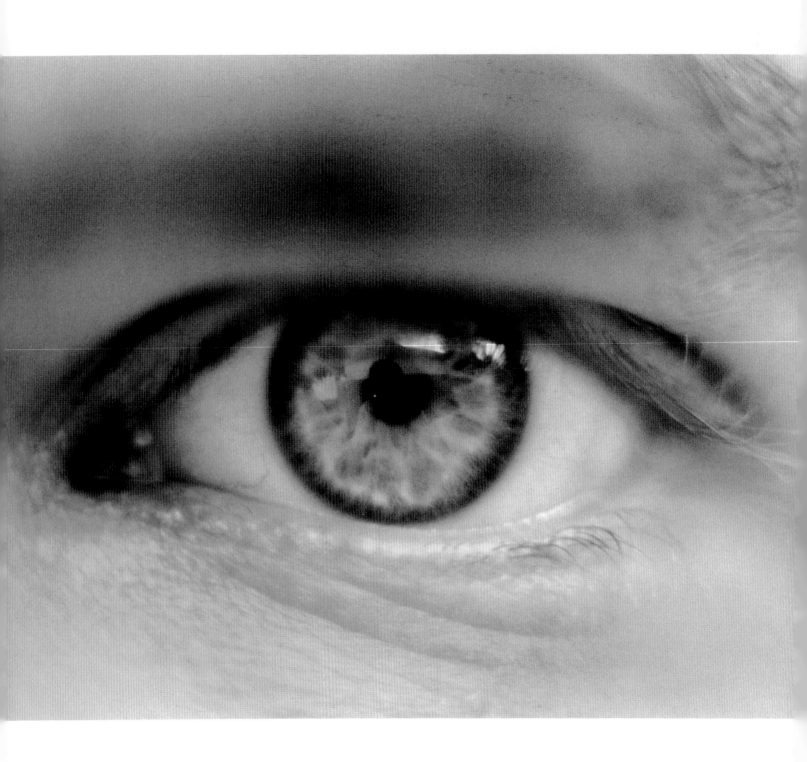

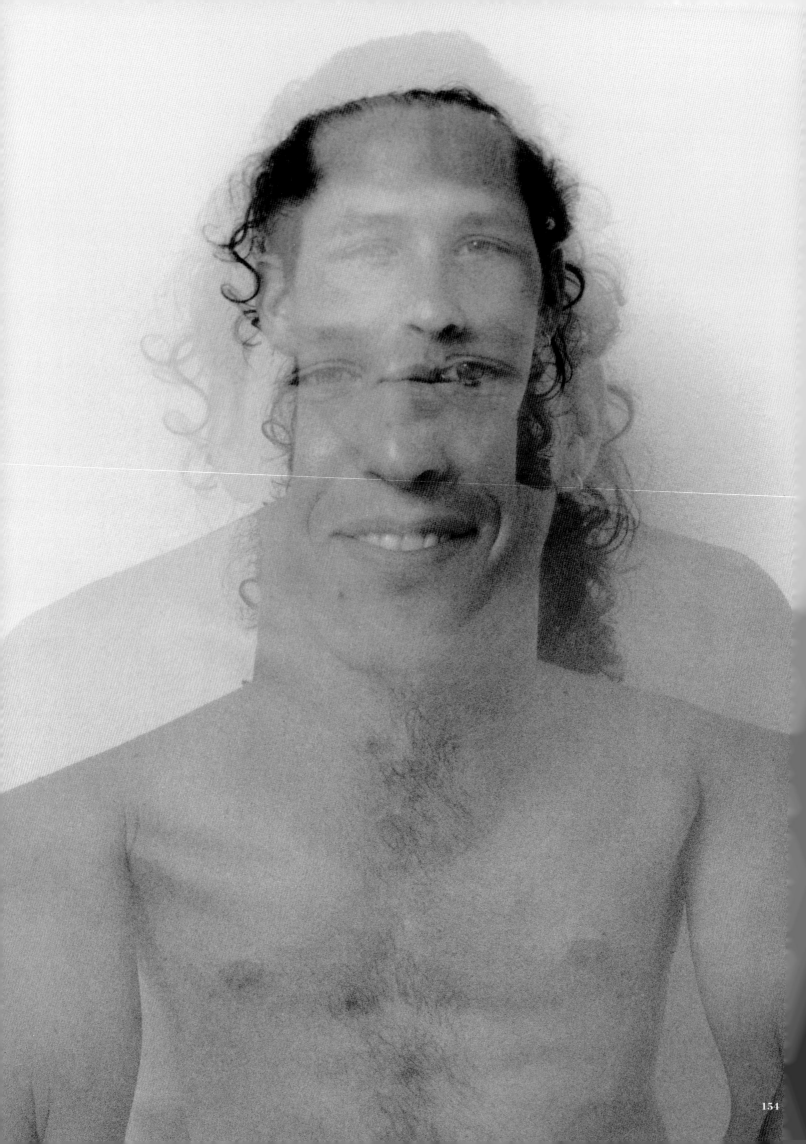

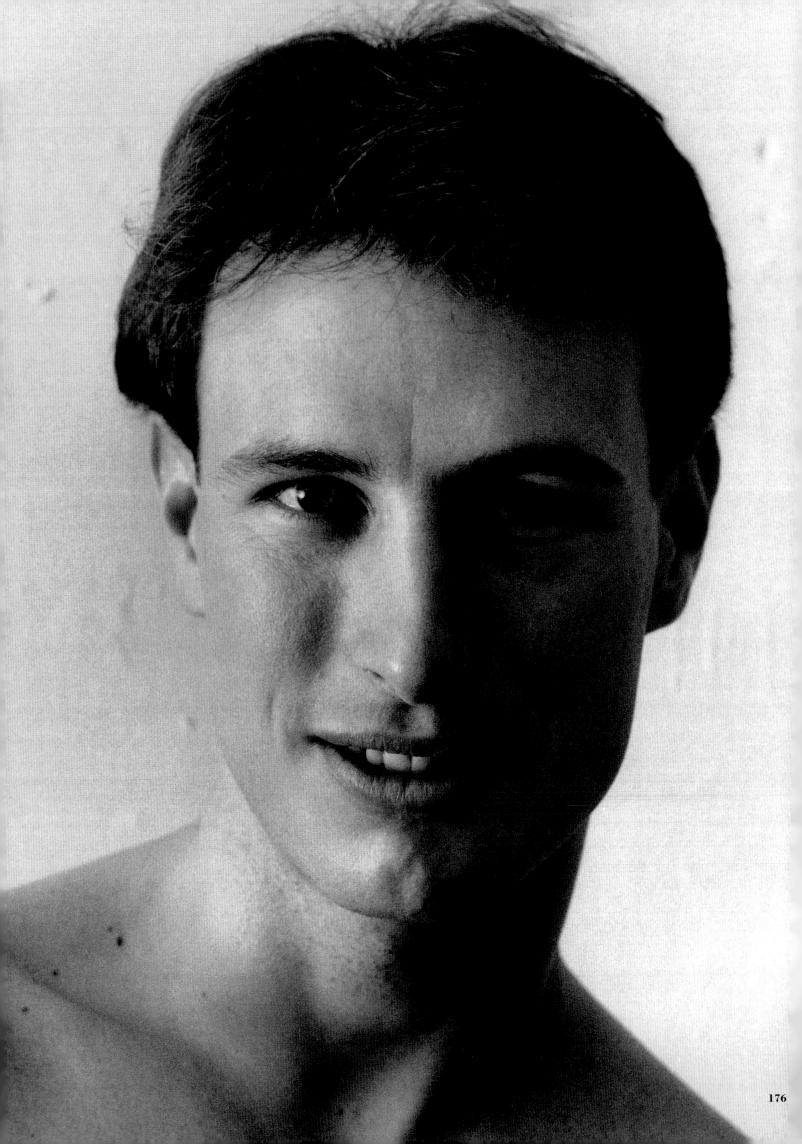

THE COLOR
PORTRAITS

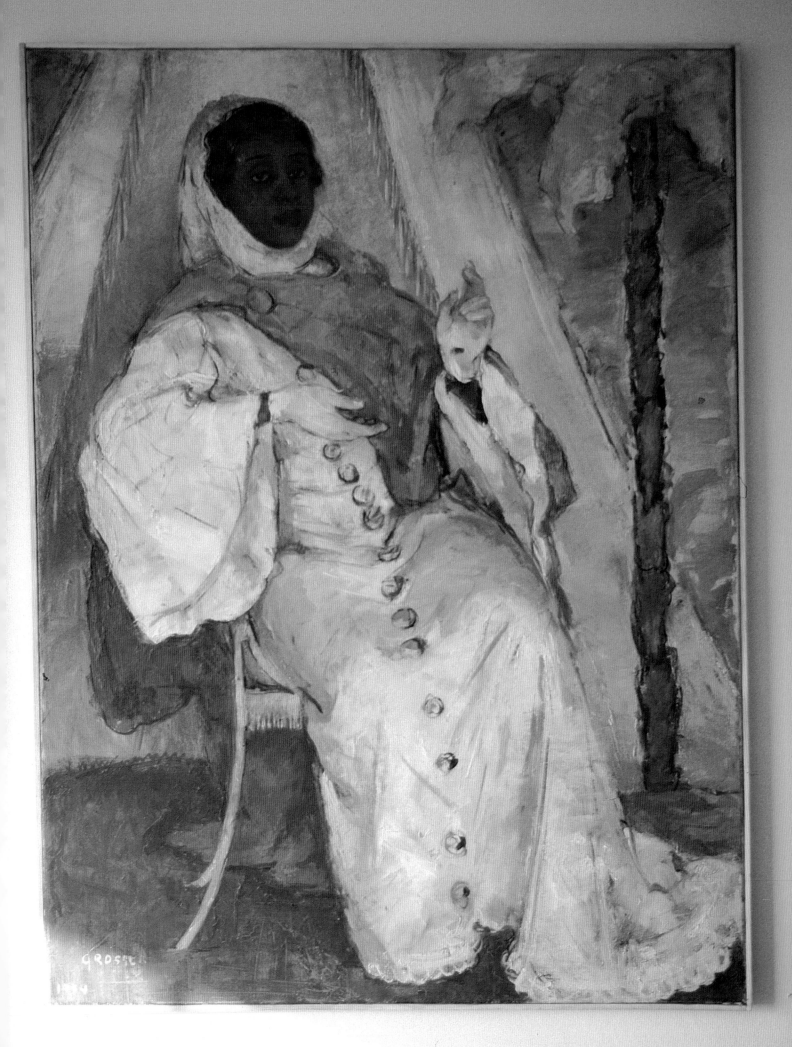

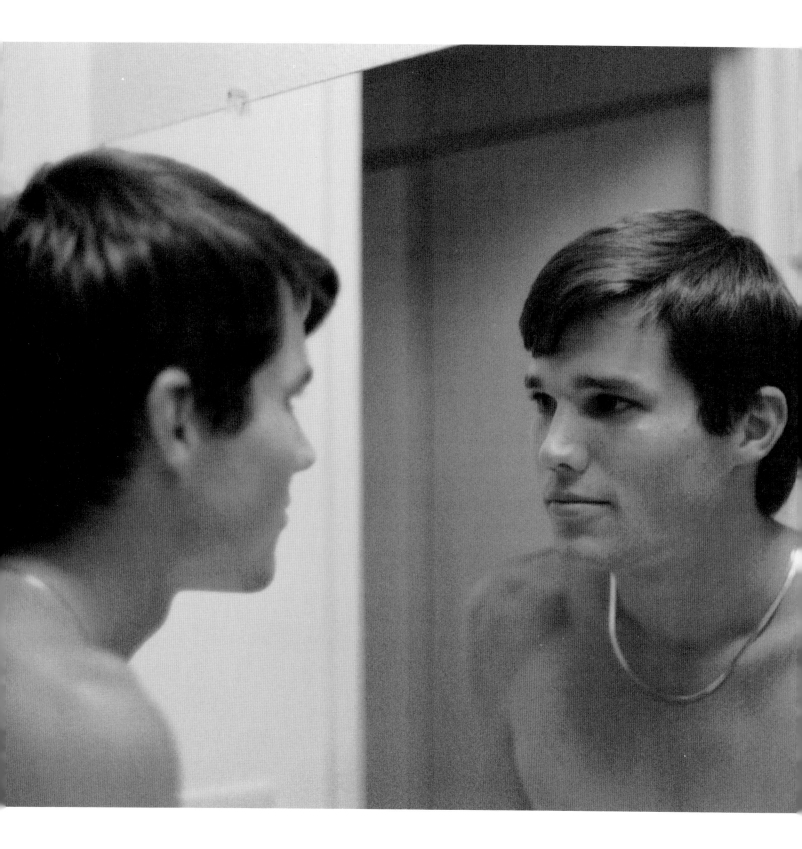

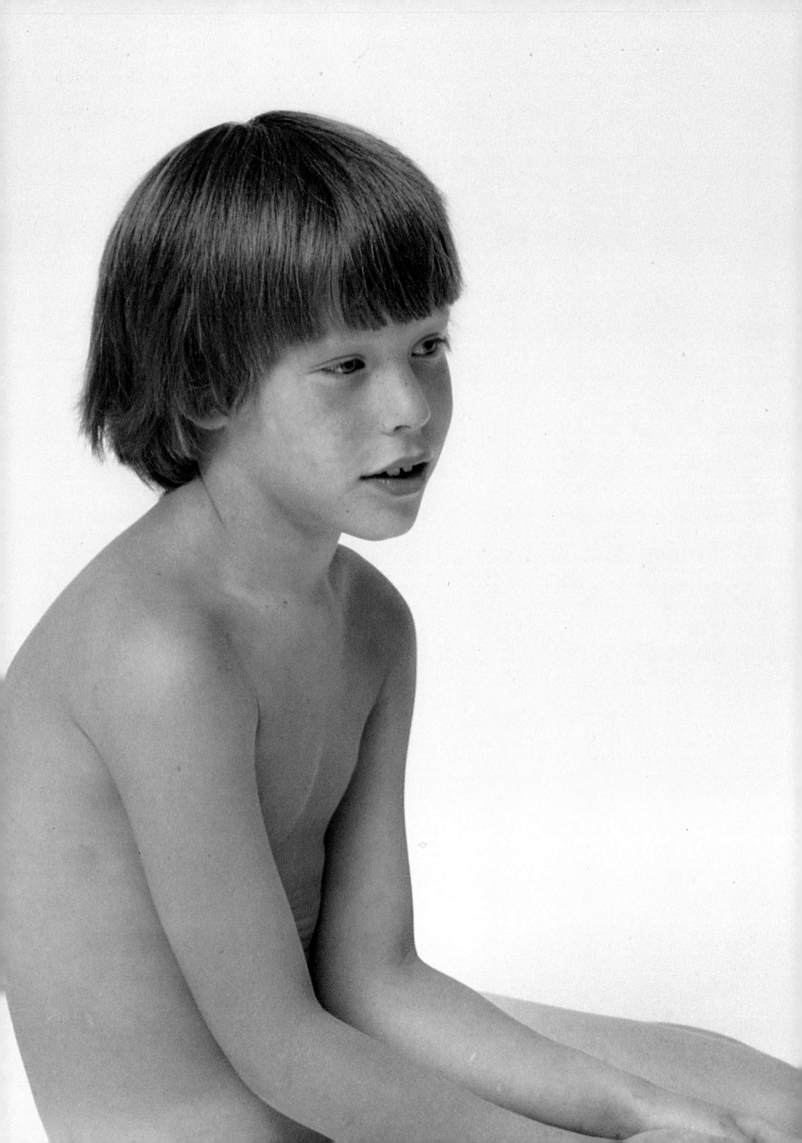

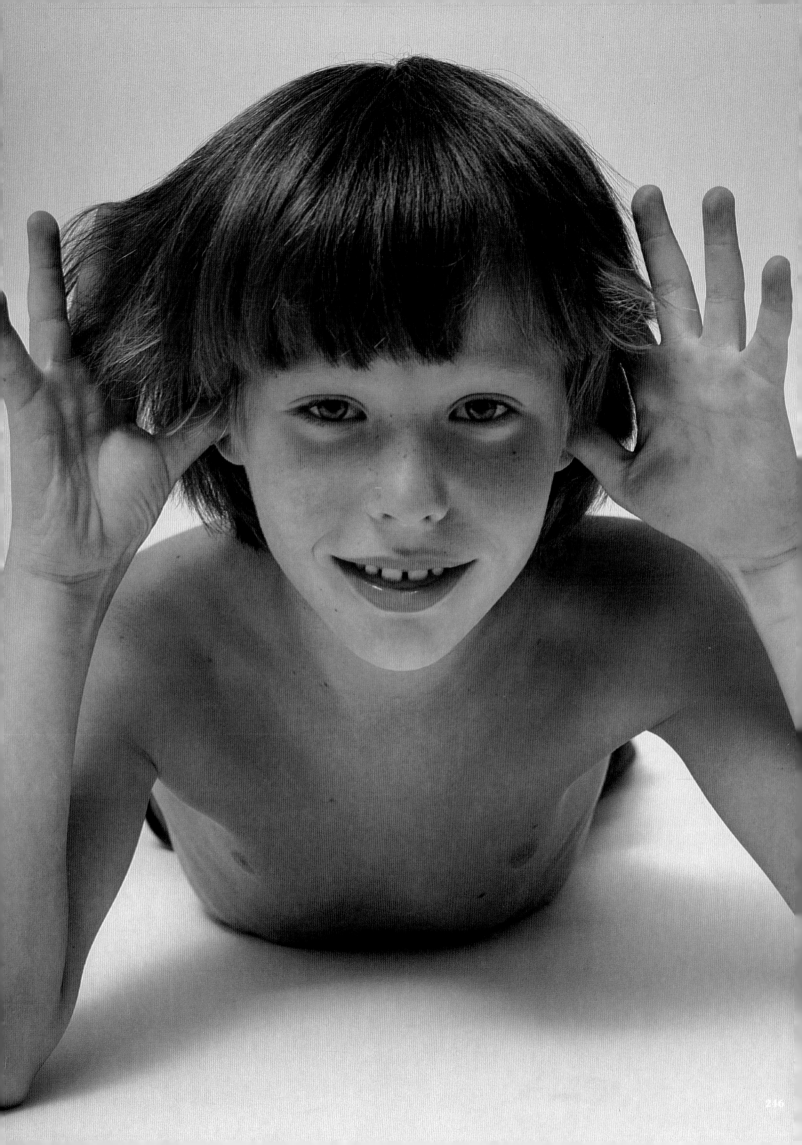

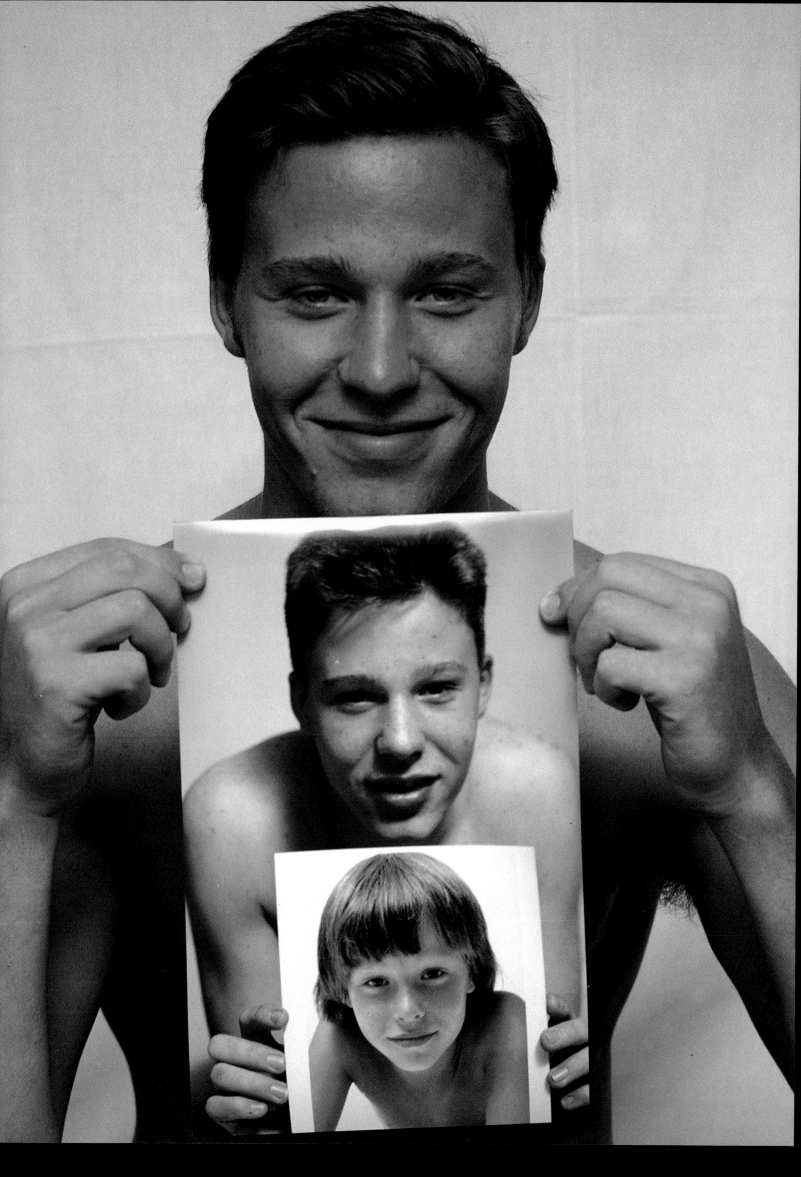

ABOUT ORDERING PRINTS

Photographic prints are available for any of the black & white photographs in this book. They are hand-printed from an internegative made from the original negative. The prints are 16 x 20, not quite twice the size of the portraits in this book. Each print has a white border and is ready for framing. My stamp is on the back, and my name hand-embossed in the lower right-hand corner. This is *not* a signed, numbered edition. The cost is $200 per print. To order, please write to the address below, or call 1-800-LIFE-101.

Although black & white looks better in photographic prints than in a book, the reverse is true of color. Hence, I do not sell color prints. If you like one of the color portraits, I suggest you remove it from this book and frame it. It will look better than a photographic print of the same subject.

❧

Please write and let me know what you think of the photographs in this book. Do you want to see more? If so, of what? Landscapes? Offbeat photos ("Fly contemplates suicide")? Nudes? More portraits? Please let me know. I'd love to hear from you.

Peter McWilliams

8165 Mannix Drive

Los Angeles, California 90046

Thank you for looking.

Take good care.

Appendix

The following are a few notes on some of the pictures. The page numbers can be found on the lower right-hand corner (near the spine) of the left-hand pages.

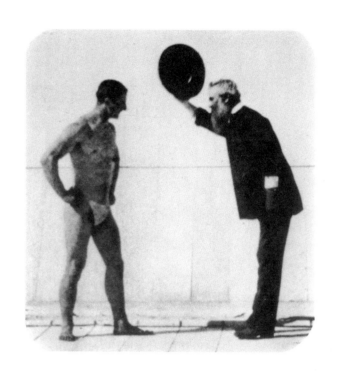

Every man's work,
whether it be literature or music or pictures
or architecture or anything else,
is always a portrait of himself.

SAMUEL BUTLER
The Way of All Flesh
1903